IF... Only Again

By the same author
Maggie's Farm (Penguin)
Further down on Maggie's Farm (Penguin)
The If Chronicles (Methuen)

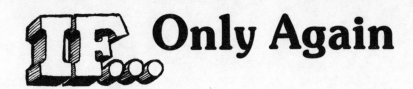

Only Again

Steve Bell

Methuen

For Heather, William and Joe

This collection first published in book form in 1984
by Methuen London Ltd
11 New Fetter Lane, London EC4P 4EE

The strips originally published by The Guardian, 1983, 1984

Designed by Brian Homer
Edited by Steve Bell and Brian Homer
Production by Brian Homer and Alan Hughes

Printed in Great Britain
by Richard Clay (The Chaucer Press) Ltd
Bungay, Suffolk

Typeset by P & W Typesetters, 202 Hagley Rd
Edgbaston, Birmingham

ISBN 0 413 56600 5

Introduction

by John Selwyn Gummer, Chairman of the Conservative Party

You know, people often ask me: how do I do it. A little while ago I was a nobody. Today I am Chairman of the Conservative Party. How did I do it? I'll tell you: I kept my nose brown and my shirt clean . . . I do beg your pardon, of course I mean I kept my nose clean and my shirt brown . . . No, that can't be right. *Nobody* wears a brown shirt in the Conservative Party. I say this with conviction because I am both a nobody and Chairman of the Conservative Party.

Be that as it may, it is with the utmost pleasure and pride that I commend this volume of Kipling's patriotic verse to you, dear reader. It is well known that Our Leader keeps a well thumbed copy of Kipling always at Her bedside table to lend inspiration at the beginning, and comfort at the ending of the day. It is to just such a role that Party Chairman, or indeed any right-thinking person must aspire if Our Leader is to succeed in Her Task of making Britain Strong Free and Great once more.

JUNE 1983

The Hereditary Principle is the very foundation of our civilisation and of Modern Conservatism. Breeding is what sets us apart. I am descended from a long line of Gummers. That is what makes me a Gummer. That is precisely what makes Viscount Whitelaw a Whitelaw. And, who knows, if our families were to form an alliance I might become Viscount Gumlaw.

490.

491.

© Steve Bell — 1983

Y'KNOW, KIPLING — FRANCIS PYM INTRIGUES ME...

OH YES... WHY IS THAT?

© Steve Bell - 1983 -

WELL.... HE MUST KNOW AN EMBARRASSING FACT OR TWO ABOUT THE BELGRANO DEBACLE, YET NONETHELESS SHE'S GIVEN HIM THE BOOT. ONE WONDERS WHAT HE WILL DO NEXT....

BOING!

....I'VE WRITTEN TO HIM IN MY CAPACITY AS PRESIDENT OF THE ANARCHO-LEFTIST PENGUIN ALLIANCE (MARXIST-LENINIST) INVITING HIM TO SPEAK AT A SYMPOSIUM. ONE WONDERS IF HE'LL COME.....

OF COURSE HE WON'T COME!

492

WHAT?! EVEN WHEN WE'VE BESTOWED HONORARY HEREDITARY PENGUINHOOD ON HIM??

YES.... WE PENGUINS ARE FRANKLY PRETTY ASTOUNDING CREATURES! FOR INSTANCE — TAKE REPRODUCTION...

I'M NOT SURE I WANT TO HEAR ABOUT THIS

DID YOU KNOW THAT AT THIS VERY MOMENT IN THE MIDWINTER NIGHT OF THE ANTARCTIC, MILLIONS OF MALE EMPEROR PENGUINS ARE HUDDLED IN LARGE GROUPS...

493

...INCUBATING THEIR SINGLE EGG IN TEMPERATURES OF MINUS 60° CENTIGRADE, IN 100 MPH WINDS. THEY SIT THERE FOR TWO SOLID MONTHS, DURING WHICH TIME THEY EAT NOTHING AND SHED UP TO A THIRD OF THEIR BODY WEIGHT?

LOOKING AT YOU I FIND THAT HARD TO BELIEVE!

© Steve Bell - 1983 -

MORE FACTS ABOUT PENGUINS— DID YOU KNOW THAT **CATCHING** AND **SWALLOWING FISH** LIKE **THIS** DOES **NOT COME NATURALLY** TO A PENGUIN??

I REFUSE TO BELIEVE THAT!

NO, I'M **SERIOUS**—YOU SEE, IN THE **WILD**, WE PENGUINS CATCH AND EAT FISH **UNDERWATER. THIS** SORT OF THING IS **TOTALLY UNNATURAL**— WE HAVE TO BE **TAUGHT** IT, Y'KNOW

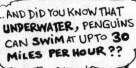

..AND DID YOU KNOW THAT **UNDERWATER,** PENGUINS CAN **SWIM** AT UP TO **30** MILES PER HOUR ??

494

....MAKES ME **TIRED** JUST **THINKING** ABOUT IT!

© Steve Bell — 1983 —

DO **YOU** KNOW THE **ROOT** OF THE WORD '**PENGUIN**'?

IN, OUT IN, OUT— **MOVE THOSE LEGS**!!

I DON'T WANT TO KNOW!

COME ON, YOU **DO** REALLY, OF COURSE YOU DO!

NO, I COULDN'T GIVE A... DON'T YOU TAKE **MONKEYS** IN VAIN, JOHN!

ALRIGHT ALRIGHT— WHAT IS IT ??

IT'S FROM **TWO WELSH WORDS** ✳ MEANING "**WHITE HEAD**". EXCITING EH??

I OFTEN GET MISTAKEN FOR **MICHAEL FOOT** IN THE **VALLEYS**, YOU KNOW !!

© Steve Bell — 1983 — .. 495.

✳ FACTS ABOUT PENGUINS FROM 'BIRDS OF THE WORLD' BY AUSTIN + SINGER, HAMLYN pp. 26-29.

9

JULY 1983

The Monetary Principle is the very cornerstone of our civilisation and the very heart of Modern Conservatism. Money is what sets us apart from the Beasts, indeed from the lower orders in general. That is why the Stock Exchange is so important to us as a Symbol. That is why we are ever thankful to Our Leader for Her vigilance, Her determination and Her resolve to protect The Money, and that is why, in this month of July, as we bask in the shining brilliance of Our Leader's smile, we know that we would rather hang ourselves than ever see Her wishes thwarted.

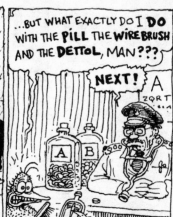

MAN, THIS IS TOTALLY RIDICULOUS!!

CRAZY 'BOUT THE THREADS, KING!!

YOU JERKS!! JUST WAIT TILL YOU GET IRRADIATED AND YOUR FEATHERS FALLOUT!! I'M A VICTIM OF BRITISH ADVENTURISM!! STUFF THE FLAG I SAY!

KING!! HOW COULD YOU??

HOW DARE YOU TALK SUCH TREACHERY WHEN HER MAJESTY'S GOVERNMENT HAS JUST AGREED TO SPEND SEVERAL HUNDRED MILLION POUNDS ON AN AIRPORT JUST FOR US!! YOU'RE DESPICABLE!!!

OUTRAGE!!

SCREW THE *@☆*☆!!* AIRPORT!! WE'RE PENGUINS— WE DON'T NEED A *☆@!!* AIRPORT!! — WE CAN'T *@*@☆!*@☆**FLY!! — REMEMBER??!!!

SHAME!

© Steve Bell 1983

STUFF THE AIRPORT!! WHY DON'T THEY DO SOMETHING ABOUT MY PLUMAGE?!! THE RATBAGS!!!

KING PENGUIN! —YOU'RE AN UNSPEAKABLE TRAITOR!!

DEFEATIST SCUM!! WHAT ABOUT THE PRINCIPLE OF SELF-DETERMINATION FOR INDIVIDUAL COMMUNITIES THAT THEY FOUGHT THE WAR FOR!!

© STEVE BELL '83

LISTEN, YOU POMPOUS JERK— THERE'S ONLY ONE COMMUNITY THAT'S COME OUT OF THIS STUPID WAR WITH ANY DEGREE OF SELF-DETERMINATION, AND THAT'S THE BRITISH ARMED FORCES!!

...AND SINCE THE ARMED FORCES OBEY ORDERS FROM ABOVE, WHO DOES THAT LEAVE WITH ANY DEGREE OF SELF-DETERMINATION??

GOD?

THE QUEEN?

MADMAN! SURELY HE CAN'T MEAN MARGARET THATCHER?

13

14

© Steve Bell 1983 — · · · 510.

Hup! Hup! HUP. HUP. HUP!

HUP HUP HUP!

O.K., ALLIES — EVERYTHING UNDER CONTROL — YOU HAVE FULL CLEARANCE FOR MISSILE TEST FIRING!

WE ALREADY DID THAT, BUB — WHO ARE YOU ANYWAY???

ME TARZAN — ME DEFENCE MINISTER — ME IN JOINT CHARGE HERE!!

HEY LOUIE — WE GOT A REAL JOKER HERE!

THUMP

TARZAN SAY: YOU HAVE PERMISSION TO WETURN TO BASE NOW!

SO LONG, YA LIMEY JERKOFF!

© Steve Bell 1983 — · · ·

HEY, TARZAN!!

HUP HOP HUP!

HUP!

...IS THIS A PRIVATE SIMULATION OF WORLD WAR THREE, OR CAN ANYONE JOIN IN??

TRAINING VITAL MAINTAIN EFFICIENCY CWEDIBLE DETERRENT DEFEND FWEEDOM!

511

VITAL EVERYONE DILIGENTLY PLAY THEIR PART IN FACE OF MOUNTING SOVIET THWEAT!!

IN THAT CASE COULD YOU DIRECT ME TO THE NEAREST SCHEDULED MASS GRAVE?

15

MR. HARDNOSE — I'M DELIGHTED TO HEAR FROM YOU. WOULD YOU JUST **HANG ON** ONE SECOND?

CONSTABLE! DON'T **HANG AROUND** HERE WITH THAT **HANG DOG** EXPRESSION ON YOUR FACE! **CLEAR OFF!!** I WANT A BIT OF **PRIVACY!!**

SIR!

502

NOW, **HANG ABOUT**, WHERE WAS I? AH YES — MY **MEMOIRS** — I SEE **NO POINT** IN **HANGING BACK** ON A PUBLICATION DATE. I THINK YOU'LL AGREE, THE WHOLE PACKAGE **HANGS TOGETHER** RATHER WELL!

...SO I'M PREPARED TO **HANG OUT** FOR A **TON OF MONKEYS** ✳ ...... MR. HARDNOSE?? ... — HELLO?? MR. HARDNOSE?? ......✳@✳✳☆☆☆✳!!!... THE BASTARD'S **HUNG UP!**

✳ 100 MONKEYS = £50,000

© Steve Bell 1983

WAH WAH!! WAH WAH!!

POLICE

BADGER

TOP THE NEXT PINKO, YOUNG JOHN!

?

POLICE

BADGER

© Steve Bell · 1983

ER...I BEG YOUR PARDON, SIR??

503

"**HANG A LEFT**" YOU **WALLY!!**

OF COURSE, SIR — I'M SORRY, SIR!

BADGE

19

PEOPLE ARE **CRITICISING** MY **POLICY** ON **CENTRAL AMERICA**, FRANCIS!!

PEOPLE ARE SAYING: HOW CAN A **COWBOY HALF-WIT** AND A **TALKING MULE** RESOLVE THE **PROBLEMS** OF THE **REGION**!!

HOWDY!

CHOFF

©Steve Bell 1983—

BUT I'VE GOT **NEWS** FOR THOSE CREEPS, FRANCIS — I'VE GOT A **PLAN** THAT'S GONNA **CUT** THOSE **COMMIES DOWN** TO **SIZE**.....

S14

I'M BRINGING A **REALLY BIG TURKEY** ONTO THE **TEAM!!**

HEY! VOT'S NEW???

HENRY THE K

RON — I HEAR YOU BIN HAVING **BIG TROUBLE** VID THE **COMMIES** IN **CENTRAL AMERICA**...?

YOU'RE **DAMN** RIGHT I AM!

HENRY THE K

I GOT **PLENTY IDEAS!** YOU VANNA **HEAR** MY **FIRST IDEA?**

SURE, SURE!

HOWDY!

MY **FIRST IDEA** IS TO **VIPE THEM** OFF THE **FACE** OF THE **EARTH** VID LOTSA **GUNS** AN' **BOMBS**, Y'KNOW VOT I MEAN??!!

UH...YEAH...ERRM.... GREAT... BUT WHAT ABOUT THE **PINKO PUBLIC OUTCRY??**

HENRY THE K

NO PROBLEM — YOU JUST **DON'T TELL ANYBODY** VOT YOU'RE **DOING!!**

MY **GAHD**, HENRY — YOU'RE A **GENIUS!!**

HOWDY!

©Steve Bell 1983-

22

AUGUST 1983

I am desolate because Our Leader is unwell. We are forced against our will to think the unthinkable; to wit: what would we do without Our Leader? Who could ever fill Her great shoes? Who could ever don Her enormous trousers? And to think that only recently I had foolishly complained that She was looking at me in a funny way. I am mortified.

27

"THIS IS IT! I'VE MADE IT TO THE FLOOR OF THE STOCK EXCHANGE!"

SNIFF
SNIFF SNIFF

"WHAT ARE YOU SELLING, CHUM?? ANYTHING TASTY?? OFFSHORE MASSAGE PARLOURS?? NUKE-IT-YOURSELF KITS??"

"NO NO!!"

"...BOUNCING BOMBS TO CHIEF CONSTABLES?? RAZOR BLADES TO NURSERY SCHOOL KIDS??"

"NO NO NO!! I'VE GOT SOMETHING THAT COMBINES MAXIMUM PROFITABILITY WITH MINIMUM SOCIAL RESPONSIBILITY!"

© Steve Bell 1983

"..I'M TALKING ABOUT DEAD DOGS!!"

? ? ? ?
?

528

"DEAD DOGS??"

"WHO ON EARTH WOULD WANT TO BUY DEAD DOGS?"

DEAD DOGS?
BUY DEAD DOGS?

© Steve Bell 83

"GENTLEMEN, YOU HAVE NO VISION, NO INSPIRATION! IMAGINE: A LARGE, UNREF-RIGERATED LORRY FILLED WITH DEAD DOGS IN THIS HOT WEATHER! — IMAGINE THAT LORRY PARKED OUTSIDE YOUR HOUSE — HOW MUCH WOULD YOU PAY THAT LORRY TO GO SOMEWHERE ELSE???"

"HMMMM!"

COO!

529

"GENTLEMEN... IT JUST SO HAPPENS THAT I CONTROL AN OPTION ON EVERY DEAD DOG IN THE HOME COUNTIES!!"

COO!
COO!

BUY DEAD DOGS!
ACQUIRE DEAD DOGS!
GET DEAD DOGS!
BUY D.D.'s
BUY DEAD DOGS!
SELL GILTS BUY DEAD DOGS!
A MARKET IS BORN!
BUY DEAD DOGS!

I FEEL I'VE **REALLY** ACHIEVED SOMETHING TODAY!

DOGBOD P.L.C.   530
DOGBOD INTERNATIONAL
POOCHSTIFF P.L.C.
THE MORIBUND HOUND Co.
SNUFFPUP P.L.C.
MORTMUTT P.L.C.
MORTMUTT EUROPA S.A.

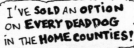

I'VE **SOLD** AN **OPTION** ON **EVERY DEAD DOG** IN THE **HOME COUNTIES!**

WHAT?? NO **DEAD DOGS** LEFT?!?

DEAD DOGS OVERSUBSCRIBED?!

HAVE YOU GOT **NOTHING LEFT TO SELL**, THEN?

AHA!

...AS IT SO HAPPENS I HAVE ONE OR TWO **DEAD DOG FUTURES** AVAILABLE!

© Steve Bell 1983

I SEE... YOU'RE A **FINANCIAL JOURNALIST** AND YOU WANT TO **INTER-VIEW** ME ABOUT MY **PHENOMENAL SUCCESS** IN THE **MARKET?** FINE! FINE!!

531.

THE **SECRET OF MY SUCCESS?** — I'LL **TELL** YOU — **FIRST** I ANALYSE THE MARKET TO DEFINE A **PRODUCT** WHICH **NOBODY ELSE** HAS THOUGHT OF..... A **PRODUCT** WHICH **IF POSSIBLE** SHOULD BE....

Steve Bell ©

...AT BEST POSITIVELY **HARMFUL** AND AT **WORST**, **NO** USE TO **MAN NOR BEAST!** THEN I **LAUNCH** IT WITH A **BIG FLURRY** AND THE **MARKET DOES THE REST.** D'YOU WANT TO **KNOW** MY **LATEST BRAINCHILD?**

-1983-

...**INFLATABLE CECIL PARKINSONS!!**

30

31

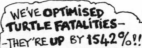

32

HOW MANY **JOB APPLICATIONS** DOES **THAT** MAKE, **KIPLING** ME OL' MATE?

I DUNNO... ABOUT **THREE HUNDRED**...

"Dear Sir, since being dishonourably discharged from the Royal Navy in 1982, I have been in and out of the slammer like a yoyo......"

LET'S BE FRANK, MATEY — THIS ISN'T GOING TO KNOCK 'EM DEAD, IS IT??!

NYGM

YOU NEED TO BE **MORE POSITIVE** — YOU SHOULD TAKE A **LEAF** OUT OF **MARGARET THATCHER'S BOOK**.......

BE ROBUST + RESOLUTE?

NO, **TELL LIES!**

© Steve Bell 1983~

I'LL SHOW YOU **HOW TO WRITE** A **JOB APPLICATION**, KIPLING — BE **BOLD**, BE **FEARLESS**, "**WHO DARES WINS**", AND **REMEMBER**, ALWAYS **TELL PORK PIES!!**

© Steve Bell 1983~

FIRST, CHOOSE THE **RIGHT JOB**. DON'T BOTHER WITH 'ASSISTANT LAVATORY ATTENDANT AT VICTORIA STATION'— **GO FOR THE BIG ONE !!**...

...GO FOR **CHAIRMAN OF BRITISH RAIL !!**

"Dear Sir, I write as a former **Admiral of the Fleet** who fought and won **a glorious victory** for this nation in the **South Atlantic**....."

"...I am a **staunch disciplinarian**, deeply committed to **financial responsibility**..."

...AND **THIS IS THE CLINCHER**, KIPLING:

"...I have not travelled on a **train** since the **Suez Petroleum Crisis of 1956**"

THEY WON'T BE ABLE TO **RESIST** AN APPLICATION LIKE **THIS**:

" Dear Sir,
I am **six feet eight inches tall**, blonde + muscular....."

"....my hobbies include drilling, obeying orders, karate and map reading....."

540

"...I eat **Trotskyists** for **breakfast** and I have a **confident** and **charming** telephone manner...."

© Steve Bell 1983

"...I feel I would make an **ideal bodyguard** for **Mark Thatcher**."

© Steve Bell 1983

You **SHOULDN'T** FEEL BAD ABOUT **TELLING LIES** ON A **JOB APPLICATION KIPLING!**.....

541.

LOOK AT IT **THIS WAY** — IF THEY SACKED **EVERY** PERSON WHO TOLD **LITTLE WHITE PORK PIES** ON THEIR JOB APPLICATION,.. THE **WHOLE** OF INDUSTRY WOULD **GRIND TO A HALT!**

I KNOW WHAT YOU'RE THINKING: LOOK WHAT HAPPENED TO THE 'MOLES' AT **COWLEY**, YOU SAY, LOOK WHAT HAPPENED TO 'RED STEPH'!

MERELY AN **ABERRATION!** — THINK OF **'BLUE MAG'** — THINK OF THE **MONSTER PORKPIES** SHE TOLD WHEN SHE LAST **REAPPLIED** FOR THE JOB!!

"THE HEALTH SERVICE IS SAFE WITH ME" M. Thatcher P.P.G.XXIAN

542

WELL, HERE I AM OUTSIDE THE REAR ENTRANCE OF 'BLUE MAG'S' BOLT HOLE...

SHE PURPORTS TO BE 'ON HOLIDAY', SO I'M JUST GOING TO EXAMINE HER REFUSE..... NOW WHAT HAVE WE GOT HERE??

...ONE HALF CHEWED COPY OF MEIN KAMPF, A CRUMPLED PICTURE OF MILTON FRIEDMAN, SOME SOILED BLUE UNIFORMS..... AHA!...

© Steve Bell 1983

THIS IS WHAT I'M LOOKING FOR: DOCUMENTARY PROOF OF THE BLUE PLOT:

"After amassing large stores of cash, C'tives will burrow their way into positions of power and influence. C'tives will then distrib- ute public cash to C'tive friends and associates...."

SECRET C'TIVE PARTY MANIFESTO

543

STONE ME!! THIS DUSTBIN IS A REAL EYE-OPENER!!

"As I sit surrounded by the sordid detritus of years of fanaticism..."

"...I muse upon the single- minded quest to destroy civilisation-as-we-know-it..."

© Steve Bell 1983

"...of the flaxen-haired punk from Grantham Lincs."

35

SEPTEMBER 1983

A bittersweet month in which I became Chairman of the Conservative party. Yet at the same time My Leader almost casually informed me that in Her opinion Doctor David Owen would in all likelihood succeed Her as Prime Minister. I admit I was a little hurt as I rather thought that I myself would be Her personal choice. Perhaps I have been unworthy of Her in some way, perhaps I deserve this; I must in future extinguish all self-conceit in my struggle to serve my Leader, my Party and my Money.

548 STAND EASY, YOU GUYS, WE'VE GOT OURSELVES A VISITOR ALL THE WAY FROM THE CENTRE FOR POLICY STUDIES IN L'IL OL' ENGLAND!

HE'S A CLOSE PERSONAL FRIEND OF OUR NUMBER ONE ALLY, MRS. MARGARET THATCHER, AND HE'S GOT A FEW IDEAS AS TO HOW WE CAN BEEF UP OUR CRAB-KILL-RATIO!!

© Steve Bell 1983

.. AS I SEE IT, WHAT YOU IN THE U.S. ARMY HAVE TO DO IS THIS:

...BASICALLY YOU'VE GOT TO TARMAC OVER EVERY CRAB-RUN IN THE ENTIRE WESTERN HEMISPHERE!!

I KNOW THAT VOICE!

549 MY NEXT AWARD-WINNING MONEY-SAVING SCHEME IS THIS.....

YOU G.I.'s HAVE GOT PRETTY NEAT UNIFORMS. D'YOU WANT TO MAKE THEM EVEN NEATER??

YOU BETCHA

© STEVE BELL 1983

HOW DO YOU FEEL ABOUT SHIRT ADVERTISING?

HERSHEY BARS

UNITED FRUIT COMPANY

YOU'RE A PENGUIN, AREN'T YOU?

AGENT ORANGE

FRANKS OT SAUCE

I AM THE BRAINIAC!

TWINKIES

39

41

558 © Steve Bell 1983

WASTE THOSE GALLOPIN' GOOKS!!

DAKKA DAKKA DAKKA

ZING

PEEYOWW

ZIP

IT'S JUST AS WELL THEY'RE STONED OUTA THEIR GOURDS, OTHERWISE WE'D BE DEAD MEAT!

ZING

I THINK WE SHOOK 'EM OFF...

NYAA NYAA NYAA NYAA NYAAA

ULP!

PHTHHARRRP!!

THE PENGUINS HAVE FALLEN INTO THE HANDS OF THE SALVADOREAN ARMY

'OO ARE YOU?

I...I...ULP... ..ER....TELL THE MAN, MAN...

559.

"MY FELLOW AMERICANS....

..WE ARE FREEDOM FIGHTERS DEDICATED TO THE STRUGGLE AGAINST BARBARISM BORN OF A SOCIETY WHICH WANTONLY DISREGARDS INDIVIDUAL RIGHTS AND THE VALUE OF HUMAN LIFE AND SEEKS CONSTANTLY TO EXPAND TO DOMINATE OTHER NATIONS!"

© BONZO PRODUCTIONS 1983

© Steve Bell 1983

...THAT IS WHY, MY EXTREME RIGHT WING PSYCHO FRIEND — I HAVE COME HERE TODAY IN ORDER TO SELL YOU A GUIDED MISSILE DESTROYER !!

44

45

47

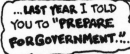
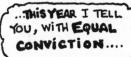

566

MY FRIENDS AND FELLOW LIBERALS....

...LAST YEAR I TOLD YOU TO "PREPARE FOR GOVERNMENT."...

..THIS YEAR I TELL YOU, WITH EQUAL CONVICTION....

....TO PREPARE FOR OBLIVION!!

© Steve Bell 1983

EVERY DAY, IN EVERY WAY, I'M BECOMING MORE AND MORE UNPLEASANT

EVERY DAY, IN EVERY WAY, I'M BECOMING MORE AND MORE ARROGANT.

EVERY DAY IN EVERY WAY I'M BECOMING MORE AND MORE OF A COMPLETE BASTARD

EVERY DAY IN EVERY WAY I'M WORKING FOR THE C.I.A.

567

© Steve Bell 1983

MEANWHILE, BACK IN PECKHAM: THE WALLIES! I DON'T BELIEVE IT!

THEY WOULDN'T DARE!! THE DIRTY BASTARDS!!

WHAT'S UP?

568.

© Steve Bell 1983

THEY'RE WINDING ME UP!!! THE RATBAGS!! NNNGHK! GAHH!! RRRRRR!!

KABLOOEY!

LET ME SEE THAT!

AHA..... I SEE..... "There is a real chance that monkey baiting may be re-introduced as Labour Party policy at next weeks conference."

NNNGHK RRRRGLERRGH!!

THIS IS SERIOUS, KIPLING— WE'RE GONNA HAVE TO CONVENE AN EMERGENCY MEETING OF THE INNER LONDON WILDLIFE FOR LABOUR BRANCH....

.. ALL ATTEMPTS TO RE-INTRODUCE MONKEY-BAITING MUST BE VIGOROUSLY OPP-OSED BY THE RANK AND FILE.......... .... ELLO, JOHN??

569

'Ello John? -JOHN 'ERE... ...AH-YOU'VE HEARD?? ...STICKY BUSINESS ...DIRTY BASTARDS... ...PROPER WIND-UP... ...MONKEY BAITING... ...THIS DAY and AGE...

TA-DAAA! ♫ THE REVOLUTIONARY PENGUIN FRONT HAS RETURNED!

© Steve Bell 1983

THIS IS NO TIME FOR INFANTILE-LEFTIST POSTURING, JOHN— WE'RE IN A BACKS TO THE WALL SITU-ATION HERE!!

(COUGH COUGH COUGH) COMRADES, WE HAVE CONVENED THIS EMERGENCY MEETING OF THE INNER LONDON WILDLIFE FOR LABOUR BRANCH (COUGH COUGH) TO EXPRESS OUR TOTAL CONDEMNATION...

...OF ANY PROPOSALS TO RE-INTRODUCE (COUGH) MONKEY-BAITING AS AN ITEM OF PARTY POLICY... (COUGH)..... ERRM...... ...WOULD YOU MIND PUTTING THAT FAG OUT, COMRADE? IT'S GOING RIGHT UP MY NOSE!!

THE MOTION I WOULD LIKE TO PUT TO THE MEETING (COUGH) IS AS FOLLOWS: (COUGH).... "THE I.L.W.F.L. REAFFIRMS IT'S (COUGH) TOTAL OPPOSITION TO ANY FORM OF (COUGH) ANIMAL ABUSE (COUGH) INCLUDING MONKEY-BAITING, PENGUIN-PURGING + MOLE-STOMPING... ..." HANG ON – I MUST JUST ASK THE ANTI-SOCIAL COMRADE

...WHAT EXACTLY (COUGH) IS HE SMOKING??

THIS IS A HADDOCK, MATEY!!

S70

YOU OUGHT TO DO SOMETHING ABOUT YOUR ATTITUDE, Y'KNOW COMRADE.....

......IT'S TOO FLIPPANT BY HALF – I'M TELLIN' YOU JOHN, THESE ARE SERIOUS TIMES WE'RE LIVIN' IN!

TOO FLIPPANT?

THERE'S A VISITOR FOR YOU, PENGUIN SHE SAYS SHE HAS A SURPRISE FOR YOU!

THAT'S COS I'VE GOT TWO FLIPPERS! ARF ARF ARF!!

©Steve Bell 1983 — 571.

GLORIA!! MY LITTLE FISH CAKE! LONGTIME NO SEE!!

DON'T YOU LITTLE FISHCAKE ME, YOU FLIPPANT LITTLE BASTARD!!

OCTOBER 1983

I'm just a little miffed with Cecil for making this year's a 'difficult' conference. Of course nobody told me anything. Gummer can clean up the mess. Gummer can explain it all to the press. Gummer can keep smiling through. Well it wasn't easy, I can tell you. Fortunately, Geoffrey quite put me in the shade over the Grenada business, his performances grow ever more dismal, yet he seems to thrive on failure. When I asked him how this could be he said cryptically; "I look bad, She looks good." His eyes then glazed over and I could get nothing else out of him. What could he have meant?

574

BRIGHTON CENTRE LABO

I SAY! YOU'RE A MONKEY, AREN'T YOU?

THAT'S ABSOLUTELY RIGHT, JOHN

WOULD YOU TELL ME WHY YOU'VE COME TO THE LABOUR PARTY CONFERENCE??

CERTAINLY — I AM THE FRATERNAL DELEGATE FROM THE INNER LONDON WILDLIFE FOR LABOUR BRANCH... (MARXIST-LENINIST)

...AND WILL YOU TELL ME WHO YOU'LL BE SUPPORTING FOR THE LEADERSHIP???

YES — IN A CITYWIDE BALLOT, THE MASSED PUNTERS OF THE INNER LONDON WILDLIFE BRANCH OPTED ONE HUNDRED PERCENT SOLID FOR ERIC!!

...AND WHAT KIND OF BLOCK VOTE DO YOU WIELD??

RTY 82ND ANNUAL C

NOT A SAUSAGE, JOHN...

WOULDN'T YOU AGREE THAT THIS WHOLE 'ELECTORAL COLLEGE' BUSINESS IS FAINTLY LUDICROUS IN THIS DAY AND AGE??

...SURELY, WOULDN'T YOU PREFER A ONE MEMBER ONE VOTE SYSTEM? WOULD THAT NOT BE MORE APPROPRIATE IN A SUPPOSEDLY DEMOCRATIC ORGANISATION?

DOESN'T THE SPECTACLE OF PEOPLE CYNICALLY MANIPULATING ENORMOUS BLOCK VOTES MAKE YOU VERY CYNICAL ABOUT THE WHOLE BASIS OF LABOUR PARTY DEMOCRACY??

YOU'RE FROM THE BBC, AREN'T YOU??

575 YES

?

TELL ME BROWN NOSE — WHO ELECTED YOUR BOSS? NOW, DO YOU HAVE ANY MORE LEADING QUESTIONS?

53

56

582.

57

584.

HERE WE ARE, THEN

RRRRRR

RRRRRRR

BLACKPOOL
100th CONSERVATIVE PARTY CONFERENCE

ALL DAY
LIVE ACTION
NASTIES
NORMAN FOWLER
IN **3D**
HEADLESS TEBBITS
TARZAN

NOW, **BODYGUARD** — WHAT USUALLY HAPPENS AT THESE SHINDIGS IS THAT **HUNDREDS OF PEOPLE** WANT TO **TOUCH MY CLOTHING**. YOUR JOB IS TO **KEEP 'EM UNDER CONTROL**, O.K.?

— © Steve Bell 1983 —

THAT'S UNDERSTOOD, CHIEF

JUST **ONE MOMENT**, MA'AM — BEFORE YOU **TOUCH** THE **YOUNG MASTER**, WOULD YOU CARE TO BORROW THIS **TEN FOOT BARGE POLE**?

YOUNG ZOMBIE

BRAVO MUM! WALLOP THOSE SCROUNGERS!

© Steve Bell 1983 —

GIVE 'EM **HELL**, MUM!

THAT'S IT, MUM — GIVE 'EM THE **BIG CIGAR** AND THE **'V' SIGN**!

585

FI-DEL! FI-DEL!!

58

AT LAST IT CAN BE TOLD: THE FACTS THEY COULDN'T SUPPRESS

THE TEBBIT DIARIES III

"I'll never forget that day as long as I live. When I heard my old pal Cecil was getting the bum's rush...."

"...I had to be there at his side, to bring what comfort I could......"

CECIL OLD CHUM — I CAME AS SOON AS I HEARD!!!

NOW CECIL—YOU KNOW I WARNED YOU ABOUT FORMING RELATIONSHIPS WITH PYGMIES!!...

586

...INTER-RACIAL SEX WILL NEVER BE ACCEPTABLE TO YOUR AVERAGE DAILY MAIL READER!!!

@☆!! *%@*☆☆ ***!!!

© Steve Bell '83

THE Tebbit Diaries

"So here I am at TRADE AND INDUSTRY, or 'EXCHANGE AND MART' as we insiders call it...... "

"...I've always been fond of selling things. I remember myself and Cecil (we go way back, y'know)..."

© Steve Bell — 1983 —

"...back in the good old days we used to jointly operate the surgical appliance stall at Conservative Party fêtes in Hertfordshire. Cecil was a bit of a smarmy bastard even then......"

COULD I INTEREST MODOM IN THIS SUPPORT GARMENT?

'ERE—FOUR-EYES! D'YOU WANNA BUY A TRUSS?

A TRUSS?! BUT I HAVEN'T GOT A RUPTURE YOU INSOLENT PUP!!

"....myself, I've always favoured the direct approach!! "

YOU HAVE NOW YOU OLD GIT!

587

THE TEBBIT DIARIES

"And so I move inexorably towards the TOP JOB. I don't mind admitting I'm ambitious..."

"...and when I look at the competition, what do I have to worry about? Certainly not DOZY GEOFF, and NIGLET just isn't HUNGRY enough, is he?...."

GEOFFREY — I'VE RESOLVED TO DONATE EVERY TWENTY FIFTH SNACK TO CHARITY!

"FOWLMAN will be plucked and stuffed long before he's ever in the running... and GUMMER — well, with a name like that he's doomed from the start..."

WELL DEAR — WHAT SORT OF DAY HAVE YOU HAD?

FRANKLY, DEAR, IT'S BEEN A BIT OF A JOHN SELWYN KNOW WHAT I MEAN?

YOU POOR THING!

"...as for TARZAN......He's just like CECIL, y'know — I've warned him time and again about associating with PYGMIES!..."

588.

© Steve Bell 1983

THE TEBBIT DIARIES

"People often ask me: 'Why do some Tory M.P's always talk in code?' You know the sort of thing I mean......."

"...those whingeing wets who start throwing around words like 'One Nation', and 'Disraeli' when they mean 'Socialist Paradise' and 'Bleeding Heart'....."

© Steve Bell 1983

"They talk in code because if they didn't, they know I'd come round and break their arms. It keeps things civilised, y'know....."

"...and of course, I do use codes myself"

589.

BY JINGO! MY SAMUEL SMILES ARE GIVING ME GYP TODAY!!

60

NOVEMBER 1983

 Michael was absolutely right to demand a right of reply to that piece of defeatist nonsense *The Day After*. And how right of him to refuse to debate the installation of Cruise missiles with that Ruddock woman or that turbulent priest, Kent. Because, of course, the real point is that neither of those two have ever been elected. I never even so much as talk to anyone who hasn't been elected, though I do allow my immediate family a special dispensation, and of course I do occasionally talk to some of my constituents.

66

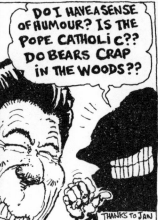

THANKS TO JAN

© Steve Bell 1983

© Steve Bell 1983

603.

Panel 1: THE FORCE IS TURNING OVER A NEW LEAF....

Panel 3: THE TIME HAS COME TO CONFRONT CRIMINALITY AT ITS ROOTS....

Panel 4: TELL ME, BOTTLER, HOW'S THE ARMED EXTORTION BUSINESS GOING THESE DAYS?

I'M AFRAID I'VE BEEN A BAD BOY AGAIN, BADGER!

604.

Panel 5: OF COURSE, THINGS ARE GOING TO BE VERY DIFFERENT BETWEEN YOU AND ME WHEN THE NEW ACT COMES INTO FORCE, BOTTLER.

'OWS THAT, BADGER?

Panel 6: WE'LL BE ABLE TO HOLD YOU FOR UP TO 24 HOURS ON AN ORDINARY OFFENCE......

ORDINARY OFFENCE? WHASSAT, BADGER?

...LIKE PETTY LARCENY, FARTING OUT OF TURN, THAT KIND OF THING...

Panel 7: ...WHEREAS ON A SERIOUS ARRESTABLE OFFENCE WE CAN HANG ONTO YOU FOR UP TO 96 HOURS.

605.

SERIOUS ARREST-ABLE OFFENCE - WHASSAT?

Panel 8: ...THE SAME AS AN ORDINARY OFFENCE - IT JUST MEANS WE DON'T LIKE YOUR FACE.

Steve Bell 1983

70

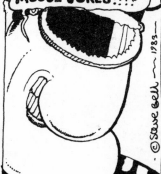

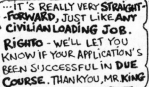

Panel 1: I SEE YOU HAVE **EXPERIENCE** IN **MINISTRY** OF **DEFENCE HEAVY** LIFTING WORK ALREADY, MR. KING...

YES

HEAVY LIFTERS NEEDED

LORRY DRIVERS NEEDED

MASS GRAVE DIGGERS NEEDED

TARZAN NEEDS...

Panel 2: ...IN THE **FALKLANDS** TOO... **JOLLY GOOD!** WE'RE LOOKING FOR **TRUSTWORTHY** CHAPS TO **LOAD** AND **UNLOAD** CERTAIN **ITEMS** OF **HEAVY EQUIPMENT**...

Panel 3: ...IT'S REALLY VERY **STRAIGHT-FORWARD**, JUST LIKE ANY **CIVILIAN LOADING JOB.** **RIGHTO** – WE'LL LET YOU KNOW IF YOUR APPLICATION'S BEEN SUCCESSFUL IN DUE COURSE. THANKYOU, MR. KING

OH, BY THE WAY – I'VE BEEN **TRAINED** IN A **HUNDRED** WAYS TO **KILL WOMEN** WITH **BEAK, FLIPPER** AND **WEBBED FOOT!**

© Steve Bell '83

Panel 4: **WHY DIDN'T YOU SAY SO BEFORE?! WELCOME ABOARD** MR. KING! – YOU **START TOMORROW!!**

612.

KING HAS SECURED GAINFUL EMPLOYMENT UNLOADING 'ITEMS OF EQUIPMENT' FOR THE MINISTRY OF DEFENCE:

STONE ME!

THAT'S ONE **MEAN** LOOKING AERO-PLANE!!

HUP! HUP! AT THE DOUBLE!

© Steve Bell 1983

GET BACK!

QUIET!

WATCH OUT!

WHO'RE YOU SHOUTING AT?!

WHAT?

WHO ME?

NO! YOU!

GET BACK!

JUMBO TWINKIES

613.

I'M ANGRY! DON'T YOU SHOUT AT ME LIKE THAT!

BACK OFF, MANIAC!

DON'T PUSH ME – I CAN KILL WITHOUT THINKING!

INCOMING WOMAN!

GET BACK!

5TH MISSILE WING TWINKIE RATION

CREESIS!

73

DECEMBER 1983

 I am proud of the special relationship this Government has with the Americans, just as I am proud of the special relationship I have with my Leader, and just as each of us is proud of the special relationship we have with our own dear Royal Family. The robust health of these relationships is, I must say, in stark contrast to the rank perversion of what some of these so-called 'peace women' get up to amongst themselves.

KING HAS DISCOVERED A COCK-UP IN THE DELIVERIES TO GREENHAM COMMON

I WONDER WHAT'S IN THESE OTHER CRATES??

HUP! HUP! LOUDER! LOUDER!

© Steve Bell 1983

AHA! THAT MAKES A TOTAL OF SIXTEEN CROCODILES DELIVERED BY MISTAKE!

WE'RE NOT JUST ANY SIXTEEN CROCODILES, Y'KNOW!

618.

NOT JUST ANY CROCODILES? WHAT ARE YOU THEN ??

...WE'RE SIXTEEN VERY HUNGRY MAN-EATING CROCODILES!!

TIME TO RETHINK TACTICS, MEN!

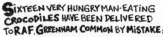

SIXTEEN VERY HUNGRY MAN-EATING CROCODILES HAVE BEEN DELIVERED TO R.A.F. GREENHAM COMMON BY MISTAKE:

WANNA EAT A WHITEMAN NOW!!

MY GOD!! THOSE CROCODILES MEAN BUSINESS!!

SNACK

DON'T PANIC! THEY MAY NOT BE WOMEN, BUT SHOOT 'EM ALL DEAD ANYWAY!!

JUST ONE MINUTE THERE, YOU LIMEY JERKOFF!

WHITEMAN! WHITEMAN! SNACK! SNACK! SNACK!

619

© Steve Bell '83

I BEG YOUR PARDON?

YOU LAY ONE FINGER ON THOSE CROCS AND YOU'RE DEAD MEAT, YOU COMMIE BASTARD!

GRAAAGH! SNACK!

WHAT ARE YOU TALKING ABOUT, YOU MANIAC??

UNTIL I HEAR ORDERS TO THE CONTRARY, THOSE REPTILES ARE THE PROPERTY OF THE U.S. AIRFORCE!!

KLIK

A DISPUTE HAS BROKEN OUT BETWEEN THE ALLIES AS TO WHO IS IN CONTROL OF A WRONGLY DELIVERED CONSIGNMENT OF HUNGRY MAN-EATING CROCODILES AT R.A.F. GREENHAM COMMON:

SNACK! SNACK!

BACK OFF YOU GODDAMN COMMIE LIMEY BASTARD!!

LOOTENANT?

I DEMAND TO BE ALLOWED TO STOP THESE CROCODILES!!

UNTIL I RECEIVE A COUNTERMANDING ORDER FROM THE PRESIDENT OF THE U.S. of A., THOSE REPTILES REMAIN U.S. AIRFORCE PROPERTY YOU COMMIE FAGGOT!!

LOOTENANT! THAT CROC JUST BIT MY HEAD OFF! LOOTENANT?

RING HIM UP NOW!!

DON'T YOU POINT THAT THING AT ME YOU COMMIE PERVERT!!

MR PRESIDENT AHEM...ER...WE HAVE A PROBLEM WITH SOME MAN-EATING CROCODILES

SO YOU'RE THE BASTARD WHO STOLE NANCY'S EMERGENCY HANDBAG SUPPLY!!

© STEVE BELL 1983

WHAT SEEM TO BE PROBLEM?

THERE'S BEEN A TERRIBLE MIX-UP, TARZAN SIR—THEY'VE DELIVERED MAN-EATING CROCODILES INSTEAD OF CRUISE MISSILES!!

TARZAN ARRIVE JUST IN NICK OF TIME!!

© STEVE BELL 1983

WRESTLING MAN-EATING CROCODILES IS FAVOURITE PASTIME OF TARZAN!!

GRUNT!

?

BRAVO FOR TARZAN!

14 HIROSHIMAS IN EVERY BITE

TARZAN SAVE THE DAY—MAN-EATING CROCS ARE A MAJOR DANGER TO LIFE AND LIMB!

TARZAN HAS BEEN DEALING WITH A WRONG DELIVERY OF SIXTEEN MAN-EATING CROCODILES AT GREENHAM COMMON

TARZAN STILL NOT LOST HIS OLD TOUCH...

...TARZAN STILL NUMBER ONE JUNGLE FIGHTE...?!

SNACK!

...PERHAPS TARZAN NEED TO THINK AGAIN...

622

...TARZAN'S GOOLIES IN SEVERE DANGER!!

SNACK!
SNACK!

MEANWHILE, OUTSIDE THE WIRE:

THANKS, MATEY!

RAF Greenham Common

623

NOW TO FIND YOUR MOTHER. - DEFINITE SHADES OF PASCHENDALE ROUND HERE!

SHLURG

SQUELCH

GLORIA!! HOW'RE YOU DOING? I HAVE TO HAND IT TO YOU LOT, STICKING IT OUT HERE IN SPITE OF THE RAIN, THE COLD, THE MUD.....

...AND THE DAILY MAIL REPORTERS.

BLEURRG

GOT ANY DIRT?

PRESS

80

Panel 1: HELLO? KIPLING?? IS THAT YOU?

Panel 2: HELLO KING - HOW'S THE UNLOADING BUSINESS GOING DOWN AT GREENHAM? / A PENGUIN RING HOME

Panel 3: FINE - IT'S GOING REALLY BADLY. LISTEN - I'VE GOT A REALLY HOT STORY HERE - DO YOU KNOW ANY JOURNALISTS? / OH SURE - THERE'S MY FRIEND BUBBLE'S HUSBAND, THEN THERE'S MY OLD DRINKING PAL RUPERT, THEN THERE'S VIC..... / I'M SERIOUS KIPLING!

Panel 4: ...WELL MAYBE I KNOW ONE OR TWO. / LISTEN - GET HOLD OF ONE AND MEET ME AT WHISSPERWHISS........ / RRRRRR

© Steve Bell 1983

627

Panel 5: THERE ARE MYSTERIOUS GOINGS-ON IN THE HOME COUNTIES....

Panel 6: THIS LOOKS LIKE THE PLACE. / THE IRATE STOCKBROKER

© Steve Bell 1983

Panel 7: KING? / HIYA REG!

Panel 8: I COULDN'T FIND A JOURNALIST, SO I BROUGHT THIS DRUNK INSTEAD. ANYWAY - TELL ME YOUR STORY - MAYBE I CAN FIND AN OUTLET FOR IT SOMEWHERE. / IT'S QUITE SIMPLE REALLY - IT'S ABOUT A THING CALLED THE 'DOLLAR CLUB' AT GREENHAM COMMON...

628.

Panel 9: 'DOLLAR CLUB'? SHAT SUMFINA DO WIF BINGO?? ERP.... / ...IT'S WHERE OUR GALLANT ALLIES ON THE BASE EACH PAY IN A DOLL-AR, AND THE FIRST ONE TO SHOOT AN INCOMING WOMAN GETS THE JACKPOT!

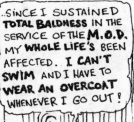

THANKS TO MALCOLM STEWART

KING IS VISITING AN UNUSUAL FAITH HEALER

NORMAN FOWLER

BRING OUT YOUR DEAD

YAY!

WHAT'S YOUR AFFLICTION BWOTHER?

I'M TOTALLY BALD AND I WANT MY PLUMAGE BACK!!

FWIENDS — I WANT YOU ALL TO TURN YOUR MINDS TO THE PLIGHT OF OUR HAIRLESS BWOTHER HERE AND WEPEAT AFTER ME....

BUPA! BUPA!!

SHAKE YOUR BOOTY!

JINGLE   CRINK

© Steve Bell 1983

635

HOW DO YOU FEEL NOW, MY FWIEND?

I'M STILL BALD, AND NOW I'M VERY ANGRY!!

SO THE FAITH HEALER WASN'T SUCH A GOOD IDEA?

NO, IT BLEEDIN' WASN'T!

© Steve Bell 1983

WAIT A MINUTE — I THINK I KNOW OF A POSSIBILITY...

SOCIALIST TRADESPERSON! SOCIALIST TRADESPERSON!!

Socialist Tradesperson

We say: TEN MINUTE GENERAL STRIKE THIS AFTERNOON

YES — THIS IS THE THING!

Socialist Tradesperson

We say: JOHN WAYNE OUT OF IWOJIMA NOW

636.

THIS IS WHAT YOU'VE BEEN SEARCHING FOR, KING!

TRADESPERSON OPINION

ALL OUT FOREVER TOMORROW!

Tradesperson SMALL ADS

ROLL-UP MACHINE FOR SALE

WORLDS FIRST SOCIALIST FAITH HEALER

86

A Cautionary Tale
for Christmastide:

THE MANIFESTO

— WITH APOLOGIES TO GEORGE CRUIKSHANK AND JOHN LEECH —

I. THE MANIFESTO IS DISCOVERED IN A HEAP OF OTHER MEDIÆVAL BONDAGE EQUIPMENT. THE HEAD OF THE FAMILY RAPIDLY SUCCUMBS TO ITS INFLUENCE.

II. THEY SELL OFF THE GREATER PART OF THEIR POSSESSIONS TO BUY EXPLOSIVES. THEY COMFORT THEMSELVES WITH THE MANIFESTO.

III.   LITTLE KEITH IS AN EARLY VICTIM OF A LAPSED BUPA POLICY.   THEY CONSOLE THEMSELVES
WITH THE MANIFESTO.

IV. FEARFUL QUARRELS AND BRUTAL VIOLENCE ARE THE NATURAL CONSEQUENCE OF FREQUENT USE OF THE MANIFESTO.

V. THE MANIFESTO HAS DONE ITS WORK. IT HAS BROUGHT THEM DEATH, SHAME AND PENURY, AND HAS LEFT THE HEAD OF THE FAMILY A HOPELESS MANIAC. THE OTHERS ARE REDUCED TO A LIFE OF VICE.

VI. THEY ARE RECRUITED INTO THE POLICE FORCE.

96

98

JANUARY 1984

 I've taken the lie detector test myself. What Saatchi's call 'sincerity testing' has now become institutionalised on training weekends in Advanced Conservatism. It's quite similar to a vigorous game of *Call My Bluff* and really can be jolly amusing. I remember once asking Cecil if he was sleeping with his secretary and that caused quite a stir. Then someone tried asking him which way the Belgrano was sailing and did he know about the Peruvian peace proposals. This had him flapping his arms like nobody's business. I must of course stress that this was only a game.

© Steve Bell 1984

643.

© Steve Bell 1984

644.

100

101

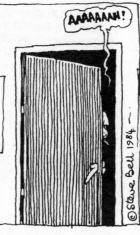

'SUNSHINE' THE POODLE HAS JUST TAKEN OVER AS EDITOR OF THE SUNDAY THUNDERBOX....

651.

NOW YOU'RE IN CHARGE SUNSHINE, WHAT I WANT YOU TO DO IS THIS....

YEP? YEP? YEP?

....TO TALK UP THE GLOBAL RECOVERY WHENEVER AND WHEREVER YOU CAN IN THE PAPER.

YUP! YUP! YUP!

© Steve Bell 1984

..Y'SEE, WHAT THE PEOPLE OF THIS COUNTRY NEED IS CONFIDENCE. THEY NEED TO BE EPSOLUTELY CONFIDENT......

YIP! YIP! YIP!

..THAT I'M GONNA MAKE A BLOODY ENORMOUS PILE O'MONEY OUTA SHARE DEALING BEFORE THE CRASH COMES!!

BOOM!

BOOM! BOOM!

652.

STONE THE CROWS!!

© Steve Bell 1984

SUNDAY THUNDERBOX
BOOM BOOM BOOM

LOOK AT THIS, KING — DEAD DOGS HAVE GONE THROUGH THE ROOF!!

SO WHAT MAN?

Dead Dogs hit Record Levels

SUNDAY THUNDERBOX business news
Everything's coming up Roses

"SO WHAT?" 'SO WHAT' YOU SAY?!? SO I JUST HAPPEN TO HAVE A WHOLE HEAP OF FISH VOUCHERS TIED UP IN DEAD DOGS! I THINK THE TIME HAS COME TO DO THE DECENT THING...

Dead Dogs hit Record

SUNDAY THUNDER business news
Everything

..TO REAP A BIG CROP O' ZLOTYS AND START A RUN ON THE DEAD DOG!

THE WORD IS OUT AT THE STOCK EXCHANGE:

GET OUT OF DEAD DOGS!

SELL DEAD DOGS!

SHED DEAD DOGS!

© Steve Bell 1984

ALL DEAD DOGS SOLD!

PHEW!

DEAD DOGS QUOTED AT ZERO!

658.

...BUT WHAT DO WE DO NOW??

RRRR

NNN

NNN

BUY AMERICAN COMPUTER DEAD DOG GAMES!!

YOW!

YEAH YEAH!

NEED NEED!

VITAL VITAL!

WANT WANT

SNOOP SNUFF

AT THE SUNDAY THUNDERBOX:

WHY CAN'T YOU WRITE YOUR OWN BLOODY LEADERS, EH? ALRIGHT I KNOW—POODLES DON'T TYPE. SO BASICALLY, THE GIST OF WHAT YOU WANT ME TO WRITE IS THIS:

654.

THE U.S.A. IS EXPERIENCING A PRE-ELECTION BOOM BECAUSE IT'S SCREWED MONEY OUT OF EVERY OTHER COUNTRY IN ORDER TO FINANCE 'SUNRISE' INDUSTRIES LIKE DEAD DOG COMPUTER GAMES. THIS WILL BRING LASTING BENEFITS TO EVERYONE.

YUP!

THEREFORE, THIS COUNTRY ALSO NEEDS A DE-UNIONISED AND FLEXIBLE LABOUR FORCE, WHICH WILL KEEP WAGES DOWN, WHICH WILL IN TURN CREATE GREATER PROFITS FOR LORD DINGO, ENABLING HIM TO INVEST IN MORE 'SUNRISE' INDUSTRIES, WHICH IS THE ONLY HOPE FOR POODLE-KIND.

YUP!

YOU'RE OFF YOUR BLEEDIN' HEAD.....AAAAARRGH!! ALRIGHTALRIGHT!! DON'T BITE MY BUM!!

© Steve Bell 1984

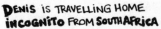

Denis is travelling home incognito from South Africa:

357

..Don't spend it all at once, chappie

JAN SMUTS INTERNATIONAL EARPOORT

Yes Baas ...tard

Ahhh...this is the life.... a bottomless G + T. And those press Johnnies haven't a clue where I am...

© Steve Bell 1984

Hello Dad!

Mother of God ...iKKKg gGGLLK!!

I'd like you to meet my entourage. Those are my detectives Dan and Stan, and this is Barry my personal press attaché!

Adger do?

Denis and Mark are flying home on business.......

Confidentially, Dad, I hear this deal's going to be simply enormous!!

Hmmm ssssllllp!

© Steve Bell 1984   358

...between you and me a little bird informed me that it's something to do with the Chinese!

Chinese? What are you talking about, lad?

I haven't been filled in on the details, but strictly entre nous it's going to be bloody gargantuan!

Don't talk nonsense, boy — those Chinese are only short little chappies — I know, I've been there!!

You silly old sod!

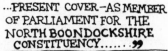

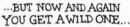

"WITH THE BACK BENCH REVOLT UNDER CONTROL IT WAS BACK TO EVERYDAY CONSTITUENCY MATTERS......

...I HAD TO PRESERVE MY COVER AS MEMBER OF PARLIAMENT FOR NORTH BOONDOCKSHIRE. THIS MEANT AFTERNOON TEA WITH THE MASSED HATS OF THE LOCAL CONSERVATIVE ASSOCIATION......

...NORMALLY I KEEP MYSELF UNDER TIGHT CONTROL.....

...BUT SOMETIMES JUST HAVING TO SIT AND LISTEN TO THEIR DRIVEL GETS ME RILED! "

OH MR. BLUDGEON...

©Steve Bell 1984

... MR BLUDGEON, DON'T YOU AGREE THAT PRESENT LEVELS OF UNEMPLOYMENT BENEFITS ACTUALLY ENCOURAGE PEOPLE TO AVOID WORK?

665

SHOULDN'T THEY BE LOWERED OR AT THE VERY LEAST, MORE STRINGENTLY MEANS TESTED?

WHAT'S WITH YOU GAGA BROADS? ARE YOU TURNIN' PINK?? THEY GOTTA BE ABOLISHED ALTOGETHER!!

"BACK AT THE HOUSE I RETURNED TO MY USUAL DUTIES......

...I AM FREQUENTLY SURPRISED THAT A LARGE NUMBER OF THE 397 MANAGE TO WALK AROUND AND BREATHE AT THE SAME TIME...

...AND SOMETIMES THEY DO ACTUALLY MANAGE TO FLUFF IT....... "

GET ON YOUR FEET, YOU DEADBEAT BONEHEAD JERKO......OOPS!

666.

©Steve Bell 1984

WRONG WAY, DIMWIT— CAN'T YOU READ??

YAH?

AYES

NOES

YAH

YAH

COME ON!! MOVE IT UP!! MOVE IT UP!!

GET UP, YOU JERKS—IT AIN'T SLEEPY TIME YET! CHEESIS!

111

FEBRUARY 1984

Quite frankly I'm fed up with the BBC and I'm damned if they're going to get away with this one. They ought to know that once a Gummer gets his gums into something then he never lets up. I am absolutely certain that there are no neo-Nazis within the Conservative Party, just as I am confident that My Leader's son made no profit from his dealings with Cementation Ltd and the Omani Government.

AT THE OFFICES OF G.C.H.Q. 2 LTD, SOMEWHERE IN ENGLAND.....

IT'S COMING THROUGH!...

CRACKLE CRACKLE

BEEP CLIK WHOOSH WHOO TWEEET

POOWHEEE GASP GASP

THAT'S IT! THAT'S IT!

THIS IS ROBIN DAY WITH FORTY MINUTES OF NEWS AND COMMENT THIS WEDNESDAY LUNCHTIME SNORT WHEEEEZE

© Steve Bell 1984

669.

INSIDE G.C.H.Q. 2 LTD, VITAL MONITORING WORK IS GOING ON.....

...IN A STATEMENT TODAY, MR. LECHIONEL MURRESA....

© Steve Bell 1984

...HEAD OF THE BANNED TRADE UNION 'SELLOUTIDARITY' SAID THAT, WHILE STATING CATEGORICALLY THAT HE WAS NOT VERY HAPPY...

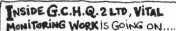

...HE WAS PREPARED TO AWAIT THE OUTCOME OF A MEETING WITH REPRESENTATIVES OF HEAD OF STATE, GENERAL JOSEPHINE STARCHER...

670.

...BEFORE AGREEING UNCONDITIONALLY TO EACH AND EVERY ONE OF HER DEMANDS!...

IN AN ANNOUNCEMENT TODAY, THE **HEAD** OF THE **POODLITBURO**, SIR GEOFFREY HOWE CONFIRMED....

...THAT **OVER TEN THOUSAND MAN-HOURS** HAD BEEN **LOST** THROUGH **INDUSTRIAL ACTION** AT THE **GOVERNMENT COMMUNICATIONS HEADQUARTERS** IN **CHELTENHAM**...

...THIS WAS THE EQUIVALENT OF 416·666 **MAN·DAYS**, OR 59·52 **MAN·WEEKS**, OR 1·14 **MAN YEARS**, OR MORE THAN **ONE TENTH** OF A **MAN·DECADE**

OR **OVER ONE PERCENT** OF A **MAN·CENTURY**, SIR GEOFFREY SAID FROM HIS **BED IN WHITE·HALL** EARLIER THIS MORNING.

© Steve Bell 1984

671.

ALL POWER TO THE KULAKS!

JOSEPHINE STAR...

IN A STATEMENT IN ANSWER TO ALLEGATIONS OF **INFILTRATION** OF THE **PARTY** BY **EXTREME RIGHT WING ELEMENTS**...

...**PARTY CHAIRMAN JOHN SELWYN GOEMMBELS** SAID THAT THERE WAS **NO EVIDENCE** OF ANY SIGNIFICANT **INFILTRATION**....

672.

JOSEPHINE STARCHER

...HE **EXPRESSED SURPRISE** AT SUCH **ALLEGATIONS** WHILST **REAFFIRMING** GENERAL **JOSEPHINE STARCHERS** COMMITMENT TO...

JOSEPHINE STARCHER

...A **SENSIBLE POLICY** OF **PROLE·CRUSHING** AND **WOG·CONTROL**.

JOSEPHINE STARCHER

© Steve Bell 1984

115

675

676

118

MARCH 1984

Lesbian-Trotsky ist- Anarchists, Miners, Treacherous Clerks: it is high time that these people felt the smack of firm government, and that's just what's happening now. You see, our entire system of government, indeed our entire Constitution is founded upon trust. When that trust is betrayed, punishment must be meted out. Only when that trust is maintained will rewards follow. That is why Nigel's first budget awarded the Duke of Westminster 300 million pounds or so, because we trust him to do well with it.

126

© Steve Bell 1984

WHAT DO YOU THINK WE'LL GET??

WHO KNOWS?

HOUSING DEPT. →

693—

SO YOU WANT TO BE REHOUSED, MR. KIPLING? WELL— DON'T WE ALL! I SEE YOU'RE SINGLE, UNEMPLOYED, AND YOU SEEM TO HAVE RATHER A LOT OF UNUSUAL PETS!...

... FRANKLY I DON'T HOLD OUT MUCH HOPE....

PETS? PETS!? WE'RE NOT BLEEDIN' PETS!! WE'RE ANIMAL ACTIVISTS!!

..WE MAINTAIN A VIABLE THOUGH UNORTHODOX INTER-SPECIES GROUPING! WE'RE AN ECONOMIC UNIT, JOHN!! I'M A RATEPAYER YOU BERK!!!

© Steve Bell 1984

WELL, I'LL SAY THIS MUCH FOR IT — IT'S GOT A ROOF!

NIGEL

BOILS RHODENT HOUSE
Accommodation for The Deserving Poor.
Opened by the Minister for Social Services. Feb 1984.

Boils Rhodent House

NORM

KEEP AND RESPONSIBILITY

694

The Resolute approach

THIS CLIMBING IS ALRIGHT FOR YOU — YOU'RE A MONKEY!! PENGUINS WEREN'T INTENDED TO LIVE AT GREAT HEIGHTS!!

SO THIS IS OUR NEW HOME!! IT'S GOT A FLOOR, WALLS, RUNNING WATER — BUT THERE'S SOMETHING FUNNY IN THE JACUZZI!!

REGINALD KIPLING — I AM FROM THE D.H.S.S. SPECIALIST CLAIRMS CONTROL AND I HAVE RAISIN TO BELIEVE YER COHABITING!

J.C.

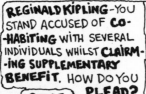

695. IS YOOR NAIRM REGINALD KIPLING?

IT IS

REGINALD KIPLING — YOU STAND ACCUSED OF CO-HABITING WITH SEVERAL INDIVIDUALS WHILST CLAIRM-ING SUPPLEMENTARY BENEFIT. HOW DO YOU PLEAD?

COME AGAIN?

I MUST WARN YOU THAT ANYTHING YOU MAIR SAIR WILL BE IGNOORED COMPLETELY UNTIL YOU CEASE CLAIRMING MONEY FROM THE STAIRT, THUS GIVING US, THE RHODENTS OF THE SPECIALIST CLAIRMS CONTROL SQUAD.....

© Steadman 1984

... ANOTHER BOGUS STATISTICAL SAIRVING ON THE PUBLIC PURRS TO OWER CREDIT.

FISH OIL

...AND THE **CHANCELLOR** HAS BEEN **ON HIS FEET** FOR AN **HOUR AND THIR-TEEN MINUTES.** HE STOPS NOW TO TAKE A **DRINK**........

..FROM A **BUCKET** WHICH HE HAS PRODUCED FROM **UNDERNEATH** THE **DES-PATCH BOX.** I'M TOLD IT'S THE **USUAL CHANCEL-LOR'S LUBRICANT** OF.... ...**GOOD LORD!**....

...**BRANDY, COLD COCOA, BŒUF BOURGIGNON** AND **DECAYED VEGETABLE MATTER**.....

...THE CHANCELLOR HAS NOW **DROPPED DOWN** ONTO **ALL FOURS** AND IS **ROOTING** IN THE **PRIME MINISTER'S HANDBAG**....

698

ONE THING **INTRIGUES ME** ABOUT **THIS BUDGET,** SIR ROBIN, AND IT'S **NOT THE FACT** THAT IT'S **JUST ANOTHER ROB-THE-POOR-TO-GIVE-TO-THE-RICH** BUDGET.....

...I'M **INTRIGUED** BY THIS NEW **ELDERLY PERSON'S PAVEMENT TAX** — THIS SHOULD GO A **LONG WAY** TOWARDS **KEEPING THEM OFF THE STREETS** AND **OUT OF** THE WAY OF **ENTREPRENEURIAL LIMOUSINES**........

DAMAGE TO WHICH HAS BEEN A **MAJOR FACTOR HOLDING BACK GROWTH** IN THE **ECONOMY.** THE **IDEA** OF A **SELECTIVE PAVEMENT TAX** IS SOME-THING **WHOLLY NEW** AND **ORIGINAL** WHICH, IN CON-JUNCTION WITH THE **ABOL-ITION** OF **MEALS** ON **WHEELS**...

...AND **O.A.P's FARES** CON-CESSIONS SHOULD BRING **PROVISION** FOR **THE OLD** INTO **LINE** WITH **CHILE** AND **THAILAND.**

GASP...**HOW DARE YOU!!**

699

...GASP... **I PEG YOUR BARDON**... WHEEZE?

MARGARET IS ON MANOEUVRE IN HER RECREATION BUNKER......

© Steve Bell 1984

702

YOU'RE DEAD!

NO I'M NOT!

GUMMERGUMMER GUMMERGUMMER!!! YOU ARE NOW!!

OK. OK!

YOU'RE PATHETIC, DOZO!! IT'S JUST NO FUN ANY MORE WITH YOU! WHY CAN'T YOU BE.... GOD! I'M SO PISSED ORF!!

DAMMIT DAMMIT DAMMIT! I'M SICK OF EVERYTHING!!

703.

HAVE YOU BEEN GETTING ENOUGH SLEEP, MARGARET?

BE QUIET, DOZO! - YOU KNOW I NEVER SLEEP!!

SMAK!

© Steve Bell 1984

DEAR GOD, IS THERE NOBODY SENSIBLE I CAN TALK TO?? WHY AM I SURROUNDED BY DOLTS??

I'M SORRY I'VE BEEN A DOLT, MARGARET

YOU'RE NOT A DOLT, GEOFFREY.. OF COURSE HE'S A DOLT! HE'S JUST ADMITTED IT, YOU DOLT!.. OH MY GOD! I'M HAVING INNER CONFLICT!!

?

704. MAYBE YOU SHOULD TALK TO A **PSYCHIATRIST**, MARGARET.... ...PERHAPS THE **STRAINS** OF YOUR **OFFICE**....

DON'T BE FOOLISH, DOZO! I WOULDN'T DREAM OF TALKING TO A PSYCHIATRIST!

OF COURSE NOT, MARGARET... ...JUST AN IDEA Y'KNOW SORRY I SPOKE AND ALL THAT........

...**I ONLY TALK TO JIMMY YOUNG**

THANK GOODNESS YOU'RE HERE DOCTOR!

TIT SOMEBODY RINK FOR A PSYCHIATRIST?

SHE'S BEEN BEHAVING RATHER **ERRATICALLY**... WE SHALL **NEVER** SURRENDER! OH GOD! CECIL! CECIL!

I SEE!

BUT **DON'T** GO IN THERE— —SHE **WON'T TALK** TO YOU

VOT DO YOU **MEAN**?

705.

...AT LEAST, NOT UNTIL YOU PUT THIS **JIMMY YOUNG MASK** ON!

134

709

135

APRIL 1984

It's quite a privilege to find myself in the War Cabinet coping with the miners strike. I've done a couple of stints of Bunker practice before, but to actually get my gums into the real thing is very exciting. My job is to supervise the overall political dimension in a coordinating capacity, with special responsibility for the government/media interface.

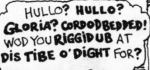

140

718.

NYAHAHAHAHAHAAAAA! "PRINCE PHILLIP OF GREECE PENGUIN"!! NYAHAHAHAAAAA!!! SHALL I CALL YOU 'PRINNY' OR WOULD PLAIN 'PRINCE' SUIT YOU??

LOOK - IT'S NOT MY FAULT MY PARENTS WERE EMPIRE LOYALISTS!!

...IT'S NOT MY FAULT THEY HERO-WORSHIPPED ROYALTY AND LUMBERED ME WITH THE SAME NAME AS BONEHEAD, BEGETTER OF BIG EARS, IT'S NO JOKE I CAN TELL YOU!...

HOW ABOUT P.P.??

ANYWAY, ENOUGH OF THAT - WHAT DID THEY GET YOU FOR, GLORIA?

IT'S PRETTY SERIOUS - THEY GOT ME FOR "WALKING IN A NORTHERLY DIRECTION WHILST POLITICALLY MOTIVATED"!

© Steve Bell 1984

WHAT DO YOU RECKON IT'LL BE? THIRTY DAYS IN THE SLAMMER?

NO, IT'LL PROBABLY BE DEPORTATION BACK TO THE FALKLANDS. THERE'S A PENGUIN PURGE STARTING YOU KNOW

YOU PENGUINS - ME - SPECIAL BRANCH.

YEAH - YOU LOOK LIKE YOU JUST FELL OUT OF A TREE!

RALLYE SPORT

I GON' ASK YOU QUESTION: "IF THERE WAS AN ELECTION TOMORROW AND YOU 'AD A CHOICE BETWEEN A CONSERVATIVE AND A COMMUNIST, 'OO WOULD YOU VOTE FOR?"

SPECIAL BRANCH

719.

THAT'S NONE OF YOUR BLOODY BUSINESS!

YEAH, LURCH - WHY DON'T YOU TELL US WHO YOU'D VOTE FOR?

UH?

© Steve Bell 1984

YOU CAN'T ASK ME THAT - S'GAINST THE FISHUL SECRETS ACT, AND ANYWAY I'M A NAZI.

SP BR

THE PENGUINS ARE UNDER ARREST......

YOU GOT PENGUINS 'ERE?

YUUURRGH

SPECI BRAN

ME...IMMIGRATION POLICE. YOU— ILLEGAL IMMIGRANTS. YUUURRGHH!

720.

GON' SENJABACK WHERE YA COME FROM, YA BLACK'N WHITE BASTARDS!

JUST HOLD IT RIGHT THERE! BEFORE YOU SAY ANYTHING MORE THERE'S ONE THING I THINK YOU SHOULD KNOW....

© Steve Bell 1984

..I CAN READ THIS COPY OF THE DAILY MAIL INSIDE 2·65 SECONDS!!

WORRRR!! THAT CHANGES EVERYFING!

Daily Mail
WE WILL OBEY MAAM

IT'S WORKING, GLORIA!!

WORRR, DEREK— —I DUNNO IF WE CAN DEPORT A 'LYMPIC STANDARD DAILY MAIL READER....

SKRAT   WORRRGH!

IMMIGRATION POLICE

'ERE....WOSSYOR NAME??

DON'T YOU KNOW ME? I'M NOTTA BLECK THE WORLD CLASS ETHLETE AND THET'S MY MENEGER...

721.

...WYATT ZONLY!

DES RIGHT! VE FROM SUDEFFRICKA END VE DON' LIKE TO GIT INVOLVED IN ALL DIS POLITICS. VE JUST VANT FRRREEDOM TO RRREAD OUR DAILY MAILS VITHOUT INTERFERENCE FROM POLITICALLY MODIVIDED BLECK COMM-UNIST EDGY TIGHTERS!!

- © Steve Bell 1984 ～

.....ER..... WELCOME TO GREAT BRITAIN, MISS.

THENKS

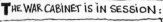

Panel 1: THE WAR CABINET IS IN SESSION: MA'AM — I HAVE ONE OF MY PRIME UNDERCOVER AGENTS ON THE LINE — HE'S BEEN SHADOWING 'THE 'ARTH' FOR OVER 24 HOURS....

AT LAST!

Panel 2: ...BUT WE NEED TO CHANGE THE RULES OF ENGAGEMENT TO ALLOW HIM TO TAKE 'THE 'ARTH' OUT NOW.

Panel 3: ..TELL HIM TO DO WHATEVER IS NECESSARY AT LAST WE'VE GOT THE BLIGHTER!

© Steve Bell 1984

727

Panel 4: ARTHUR SCARGILL — I AM ARRESTING YOU BECAUSE YOU ARE IN DIRECT CONTRA-VENTION OF SECTION 3 OF THE OFFENCES AGAINST THE HAIRSTYLE ACT 1984 WHICH I HAVE JUST MADE UP IN MY HEAD!

Panel 5: BADGER TO WAR ROOM — — IT DIDN'T WORK! —

© Steve Bell '8

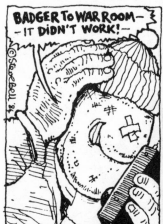

Panel 6: ...I SUSTAINED SEVERE STRUCTURAL DAMAGE WHILE ENDEAVOURING TO TAKE OUT 'THE 'ARTH' — OVER

'ERE — CONSTABLE — GET ME A JOURNALIST WOULD YOU?

DON'T YOU MEAN AN AMBULANCE, SIR?

Panel 7: NO, I MEAN A JOURNALIST, YOU BERK — — I WANT PICTURES OF THIS OUTRAGE SPLASHED OVER ALL THE PAPERS. THE SUBHUMAN VERMIN WHO DID THIS ARE GONNA SUFFER!

728

Panel 8: GORDON BENNETT! NOW SOME HEARTLESS BASTARD HAS GONE AND STOLEN MY HAT!!

I WOULDN'T TALK TO THE CHIEF CONSTABLE JUST NOW IF I WERE YOU—HE'S IN A BIT OF A **BAD MOOD**.

GRRZZRRMGGRRR BGGRRRFGGRNNZR GRZZRRR...

..HIS **MONKEY** REFUSES TO TALK TO HIM, AND NOW HE'S JUST **FAILED** TO MAKE THE **ARREST** OF THE **DECADE**. HE'S VERY **BROWNED OFF** INDEED....

GRRZZRRR... IT'S **TRUE** WHAT JOHN THE MONKEY SAID, YOU KNOW...

...I'M JUST A BLEEDIN' **LACKEY**. I SHOULD HAVE **LISTENED** TO **MY OLD MOTHER** WHEN SHE USED TO SAY TO ME:

729.

"SON, IF I EVER CATCH YOU JOINING THE **FILTH** I'LL **NAIL** YOUR HEAD TO THE **FLOOR**."

© Steve Bell 1984

I DON'T WANNA BE **SPAT AT** AND **VILIFIED**. I DON'T WANNA BE **SNEERED AT** AND **SWORN AT**...

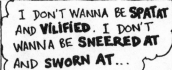

I WANNA BE **RESPECTED**. I WANNA BE LOOKED ON AS A **FRIEND IN TIME OF NEED**.

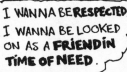

730.

I JUST WANNA BE **LOVED**!

...AND I WANT **ANY OTHER ATTITUDE** TO BE **ILLEGAL**.

© Steve Bell 1984

MAY 1984

I must say I feel a little confused. It turns out that I have not been in the Command Bunker at all. I have been sitting in the wrong bunker for three weeks. What is more ominous is that Cecil is generally raising his profile all round and has even gained access to the Command Bunker proper. It is a bit thick. I'm definitely going to raise the matter with the Leader as soon as I find out where she is. To make matters worse several American Secret Servicemen have been extremely rude to me.

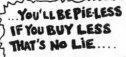

"HE'S ON HIS WAY TO HEAVEN IN A PIE"

...THERE'LL BE NANCY'S FIVE HAIRSTYLISTS IN THAT PIE....

733.

...YOU'LL BE PIE-LESS IF YOU BUY LESS THAT'S NO LIE....

...THERE'LL BE NO-ONE THERE TO RILE US NOBODY WILL BE TIE-LESS...

...WE'LL HAVE NO UNWHOLESOME WILDNESS IN THAT PIE!

© STEVE BELL 1984

YES, HE'S ON HIS WAY TO HEAVEN IN A PIE:

THERE'LL BE MAJOR BOB D'AUBUISSON IN THAT PIE....

...'COS HE'S A MAN THAT LIKES TO HELP FOLKS DIE

© Steve Bell 1984

...THERE'LL BE MAJOR BOB D'AUBUISSON —DEATH'S PALM HE'S BEEN A-GREASIN...

...YES THAT KILLER WILL BE SEASONIN' THAT PIE!

734

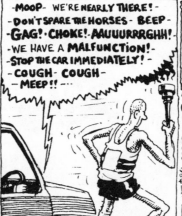

THIS SECTOR SPONSORED BY

ELDERLY **Mac**

...THERE'S A DIFFRENCE WITH MACGREGOR HE'S A DIFF'RENT KINDA MAN....

♪ ...HE CHOPS UP ENTIRE INDUSTRIES AND SHOVES THEM DOWN THE PAN....

...HE'S BEEN FALLING OVER BACKWARDS TO GET THE WORKFORCE OFF THE HOOK COS THE SUREST ELECTRICITY COMES FROM CHINESE COAL + NUKES!

745.

THIS SECTOR SPONSORED BY:

"IT'S THE REAL THING..."

746.

"C.I.A."

"...WHAT THE WORLD WANTS TODAY..."

"Covert Action"

153

HELLO? GLORIA?? I'VE GOT SOME **BAD NEWS!** **KING** AND **JOHN** THE **MONKEY** HAVE JUST BEEN **SEIZED!!**

WHAT'S THAT YOU SAY? SHOVED IN **DUFFEL BAGS** IN **BROAD DAYLIGHT??** DEPORTATION?? THAT'S **OUTRAGEOUS!!**

© Steve Bell 1984

HELLO? GLORIA? GLORIA? ARE YOU THERE?

751.

© Steve Bell 1984

...ALL MY FRIENDS **SEIZED!!** WOMMA GONNA DO WIVOUT EM?

752.

...AVENUVVER SHRINK... WHY NOT? SSSSLLP SSSSLLP SSSSLLP GLUG...

I JUS CAN'T **BLEEVE** MA PENGUINSH ARE GONNA BE **KICKED OUT** THE COUNTRY! I THIG I'M GONNA **CRY!!**

THE 96 HOUR DETAINEE

GOTTA SHAKE OFF THISH **DEPRESSION** GOTTA DO SHOMETHING POSNITIVE T'TAKE ME MIND OFF IT!!

THISH ISH JUSHTA THING! GET SHTUCK INTO A GOOD FOO'BALL MATCH!!

NOW ON: **BILLY GRAHAM** -V- THE **GODLESS HORDE**

FIXTURE LIST
BILLY GRAHAM -V- LOIS PULAU
BILLY G... -V- JOHNNY BIRAN...
BILLY ... -V- JOHNNY POPO

PORT VALE! PORT VALE!! WO WO WO!!!

MY FRIENDS...

WASHA SHCORE MATE??

SHHH!

© STEVE BELL 1984

MY FRIENDS— I WANT YOU ALL TO ASK YOURSELVES A SEARCHING PERSONAL QUESTION...

...DO YOU KNOW GOD REALLY AND TRULY? IF YOU CAN'T ANSWER THAT QUESTION, I CAN HELP YOU NOW...

REFEREE'S GETTIN' A BIT CARRIED AWAY ISHN'T HE?

...FOR I DO KNOW GOD PERSONALLY. HE IS A FREELANCE COMMODITY BROKER AND SECONDHAND CAR SALESMAN AND HE LIVES IN A BIG HOUSE JUST OUTSIDE OF NORMAL, ILLINOIS!

753.

MY FRIENDS, I'M GOING TO ASK YOU ANOTHER DEEPLY PERSONAL QUESTION...

WHENZA FOO'BALL GONNA SHTART?

...DO YOU REALISE THIS, MY FRIENDS— EVERY SINGLE DAY EIGHTY THOUSAND PEOPLE ARE FLATTENED BY BEER TRUCKS BEFORE THEY'VE EVEN HAD A CHANCE TO CHANGE THEIR UNDERWEAR?..

FRIENDS— I'M GOING TO ASK YOU THIS— DOES YOUR UNDERWEAR MEET WITH THE LORD'S APPROVAL?

© STEVE BELL 1984

754

YAY YAY!!! I SEE THE LIGHT! MY UNDERPANTS ARE SAINT MICHAEL'S UNDERPANTS!!

PRIZE THE LARD!

157

THE BOTHA BROEDERS ARE GOING TO PLAY DOWNING STREET:

COOL IT, KREP MAN - THIS IS THE BIGGEST GIG OF THE DECADE. WE DON'T WANT TO MIKE A BED IMPRISSION!!

BARP

NYAAA, PIG MAN, YOU WORRY TOO MUCH - IT'S GONNA BE A PIECE OF CIKE, AREN'T I RIGHT, WENK?

DES RIGHT, KREP

- HEY DIRT MAN - - TELL PIG HE'S WORRYING ABOUT NOTHING - I CAN'T CONVINCE HIM!

'E'S RIGHT, Y'KNOW PIG - WE CLEAN WHOLESOME BOYS. WE NOT GOING TO DO ANYTHING ENTI- -SOCIAL, ARE WE?

YIH!

DES RIGHT - -'ERE, DIRT YOU GOT MY BLECKSKIN TROUSERS ON!?

THE BOTHA BROEDERS ARE COMING

YOU PRISS GINTLEMEN MUST REALISE THET WE'VE CLEANED UP OUR ECT COMPLETELY SINCE THE OLD DAYS...

..DES NO MORE MOWING DOWN THE AUDIENCE... ..DES NO MORE HENGING KEFFIRS ON STAGE..... ..WELL, NOT SO MUCH ANYWAY....

YES, AND WE EVEN HEVE A COLOURED IN THE ECT THESE DAYS...

'E'S OUR IN-FLIGHT WINDOW CLEANER!

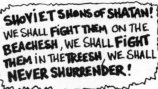